Pain Songs

Pain Songs

Daniel Sluman

Nine
Arches
Press

Pain Songs
Daniel Sluman

ISBN: 978-1-916760-38-7
eISBN: 978-1-916760-39-4

Cover artwork: Jean Baptiste Marc Bourgery, *Traité complet de l'anatomie de l'homme: comprenant la médicine opératoire* (Band 6, Atlas). Paris 1839. Heidelberg University Library.

First published May 2026 by:

Nine Arches Press
Studio 221, Zellig
Gibb Street, Deritend
Birmingham
B9 4AU
United Kingdom
www.ninearchespress.com

Printed on recycled paper in the United Kingdom
by Imprint Digital.

Nine Arches Press is supported using public funding
b

Supported using public funding by
ARTS COUNCIL
ENGLAND

for Emily always

Contents

Heatwave, 2021

neighbours argue & fuck
through the thirty-degree heat

as we smoulder
in our musty room

the perfume we douse
on the sheets

the mattress too heavy
to turn

& the curtain we fuss like a wound

all summer
we order pizza & push back

each other's cuticles

until we can't tell
whose fingers are whose

your armpits left
to stubble into july

the red you paint my nails

half-awake
as the days smother and fray

each night the bulb in the hallway
sputters a ragged breath

until you twist it loose
in your palm

pulling darkness through the flat
as I wash your mooncup

at the sink
whilst you sleep

the pearls of pink
drip down my wrist

face lost in the mirror

as I place it back
on the porcelain

pristine each night

Atopic Dermatitis

just like the trees that burst apart
in long summers like these

dismantling the forest's quiet joy

I have found my body breaking
over basins

& bathroom floors

my nails at my flesh
as the blood rises to the surface

tacky & sweet
like a spoiled peach

knuckles slick when I wake

having scratched myself open
in the crux of some dream

the smudged petals I leave
on the sheets

that you've learnt

to blink over with dye
stripping constellations

that map a path back
to a childhood

doused in grease

& wrapped in swathes
of sodden gauze

for thirty years
I have been open-mouthed

at the mechanics
of this body

the heart's steady cinch
& my world dripping

through my fingers

amazed at how little
I am able to keep

of this life within me

Chronic

god whispered in my ear

but the only word I caught
was *pain*

lord I have learnt
to suffer well

to keep silent

as the lit nerve stirs my body
into meaning each morning

it begins
like a murmur

gathers itself
into a loose gust pushing

the window open

& say I understand the lesson
this life has taught me

to know myself
to the root of each hair

to cherish this feeling

pale & seized around the suffering
I'm drunk on

well what kind of surrender is this ?

crumpled in the footwell
        of my father's car

as he drives me to the hospital

        how do I explain
                how lucky I am

to be the husk this life passes through
        like a sweat or splinter

how I hang over myself
        in bed at night

& watch the pain climb inside me
        whilst I sleep

& if there is faith
it is the faith required

to keep waking inside
        this immovable reality

this ache that tells me
        to love loudly

                the body on fire

On leaving the pain clinic

summer was over

I watched the light
in the building

slip clean
from the windows

darkness resting

over steel drawers
filled with scalpels

rolls of gauze
& tiny bottles of anaesthetic

the storm clouds spilled over
the slick

of afternoon traffic

the sensation of a lit cigarette
pressed into my left hip

kept me here in the car
rain sifting through hedgerows

the knowledge of my pain
always intact

this stubborn sense

that I will forever
be wedged between the life

we're making

& the one we've carefully set
aside

at the interchange
my mind drifts to thoughts

of you in your dress
of orange flowers

when I am pulled whole
through the cotton

by the noise

of the truck's wheels
swerving before me

the spray

of water lifting my car
off the road

held momentarily
neither in pain or at ease

between the ground
& the air

The accident

because I love you too much

to die
without you

I curl up
against your back

in bed
as you snore

having realised
I doubled my dose

half-dreaming fingertips
slipping over the pills

in the dark

now it's just me
& the screen of my phone

as I force myself awake
through the night

fingers pressed against my neck
as I check my watch

searching my body

with a curious terror
for the point

where sensation turns

for the moment
I must ring the ambulance

& wait
for the soft blue lights

to spill through
the window & over

our sheets

MRI

like a man about to travel
a great distance

I slide my wallet
& wedding band into the tray

the tired smile
& warm hands of the nurse

who straps me
into the stretcher

before I am drawn
into the open mouth

of the truth again

you split my vertebrae
into a thousand frames

& show the pale crease

where the disc bulges
into the spine

& spills me
from the tangle

of thoughts
I am reaching for

twenty years ago

you saw the bend in the road
before I was forced

to bow down to it

my diviner
of possible deaths

my future cut out of air

The Hickman line

I spent the last summer
of my childhood

dying
inside a hospital room

& because children
are not meant to be buried

because my body

had grown numb
to the language of the doctors

& their best-case scenarios

they threaded a line
from my rib

to my heart

a telephone installed
in the hope we could talk

to the end
flowering inside me

the first time it slipped loose
droplets of saline

like gravel lit
on the x-ray

the second line raised yellow crystals
at the entry site

& had to be pulled
before the infection crawled

into my chest

now nothing remains
of that year

just the white pucker of scar
on my side

that your fingertips circle
& snag

when we're wrecked beside
each other

eyes upturned
as if you're feeling

all those days of sunshine
I never knew

from behind
this fibrous blotch

of flesh

this tight knot
I am too terrified

to unpick myself

Surgery

I've been passed
through the hands

& eyes

of strangers
like a prize or blessing

& the truth is

my body
has never made more sense

than when I'm not
inside it

I have lost count
of the men & women

who have scrubbed
my limp body clean

in rooms filled
with artificial light

eyelids taped shut

consciousness flung
from the building

all my loves & hopes
deferred

Post-surgery

all night I've been waking
to the sound of moths

striking the window

of our kitchen
like scattered applause

each gentle thud jolting me
from dreams of drowning

on our dusty sofa

pinching open the edges
of this wound

stripped lengthwise
down my back last week

under a tide of propofol
that pressed me down

like a dozen gloved hands

the layers of fat rippling
in the golden light

either side of my spine

a part of me still
swimming

in that place
where the nurse slapped

my forearm to chase
the pulse with her forefinger

a void where numbers
& logic fall away

where all the words
& feelings I've held back

breathe

The matching tattoos

I pull up beside you in the sheets

        & we trace the fresh edges
                of the new tattoos

        how this wasn't our first time

we still honour the marks
        we carry

                from a past

        staring at ceilings in rooms
                we can't remember

with a different name
        between our lips

        the way the blood misted
                & rose to the surface

                of our skin

the post-coital pearl of black
        straining over the needle's tip

        & your fists paling
into the leather of the chair

        every *I* a steel rail
        hammered

on a track we'll travel
        together

whatever distance tries
to press us apart

that pain a reminder
of what it is to stand

by this life we practise

the tenderness that floods
the body after the hurt

& the privilege to lie
against you here in bed

newly printed & shaking
in a windowless room

how the wounds we wear

on our sides look like mouths
kissing

over the cellophane

Honeymoon

we drank too much wine
& fell up the stairs

to our room

hung over
the edge of the land's knowing

we spat into the Atlantic
& watched it cut re-cut

itself against the beach

the tide's quiet promise
to pull us

into nothing

to strip us of our clothes
our jewellery

grind our doubts into sand

the ivory lingerie you buried
like a body

under the bed
for this weekend

how for three nights we lived
& loved

against our proximity to the past

we watched the terms
of our single lives slip

through the ocean's pane

late-night on a bench
in the harbour

fish & chips burning in our laps

& framed by the headlights
of our car

behind us

gold rings spilling
into the dark

Sustenance

half-awake
& empty as a saint

I grieve for taste
under a tide of opiates

for the slicked lips
& rounded mouth of appetite

my love language is
being survived

by the work of your hands

their relentless labour
sustaining the engine of my heart

the way you frisk my body
for the pain

that buries my hunger from me
& three times a day

you bring my life to me

white wine poured
into melting butter

the sweetness of garlic
warming in fat

in our last few years
of sloppy joy

you've been feeding

the tiny flame of my appetite
higher

half-sunk in the sheets
as you wrap rice

in foil for tomorrow

there is such kindness
& imagination

in this world

& so much of it sings
barefoot

in my kitchen

Corpse flower

you let yourself be led
closer always

to that note
caught somewhere

between fresh shit
& rotting fish

wedged in the duvet

your limbs burning
in the sheets

the mind an alarm
that rings & rings

you do not care

what is bitter
& what is sweet

what brings life
& what expels it

swept
head to toe

through a field of blossom

each petal the colour
of blood crackling open

in the sunlight
of your imagination

& perhaps
you put the creased corolla

to your lips perhaps
bite the stem somehow

we still pretend
we are sniffing the idea

of a flower through
the bloom & not

that it is the purse-
soft anther

the green stalk & shaking grain

of pollen itself
that is drawn through

the open window
of the body

Mould

& how can we be angry
at this silent partner

looking to lie between us
in the sheets

a stranger
carried into our lives

on the back of the breeze

bled through
gaps in the mortar

now we cannot seize
the part of our minds

that see omens
in the wall

it ticks behind our eyes
at night

where I dream of the fuzz
stiffening like reeds

through the wet mucosa
of my lungs

each day we wake
inside its mind

this singular hum

this pair of green hands
running up the walls

Silver maple

this is how it must feel

rotting
from the inside

there is a ache
& it does not stop

we do not know why

we are brittling
in the wind

but the stiffness
the burn accumulates

like a debt or plaque

& I hadn't noticed
until I could not

not notice it anymore

from a certain way
of thinking

I should be tenderly
pressing

my bones against
the edges of a cold box

sometime
before the millennium

yet I stand here

the accrued fractions
of ever unlikely propositions

& maybe this is why
my body sobs

in confusion

maybe it is happiness
mistranslated

as the messy living
I should never

have been afforded

Ceilings

just as the night sky shifts
beyond the minds

of the animals outside

the ceilings
we are pressed beneath change

in aspect & colour

each evening they drop
a little closer

in rooms that carry us
from one year

to the next

we float below water stains
& cracks

lit like reels of stars

my faith
in a better reality frayed

to a single thread

as I scan the cobwebbed beams
in silence

& wait for a sign
that refuses to drop

lidocaine-bright
or yellowed from bowers of smoke

some nights only darkness seems
to keep the roof up

& each evening
the quietness wraps

a little tighter
as we sink into the sheets

eyes dazed shut

our prayers like hands
crawling

over the drips of faux-plaster

how our shirts slip from one colour
to the next

& time is always in deficit

catching up or catching on
to something half-gone

Meditation

the light rolls over me

& I follow it
as it eddies & spills

tumbles over the flickers
of tension & dread

that curl like embers
extinguished

in an upturn
of air

this pain always blooming
or rotting

rotting
or blooming

its roots weave
around the vertebrae

to tighten
& I name it all

each feeling

I pare the fascia from the cartilage
cut the muscle from the bone

& let every part
live

the diaphragm's slow flexion
filling my lungs

until each cell is flush
& I am a steady beat

a throb of light in the dark

when I tense my left hip
the mind pulls

the imaginary leg upwards

like the mast of a ship
in a bottle

& if this can be made real

if I can feel the limb
that was taken from me

two decades ago

cramping under a blanket
in south london

who's to say

the beloveds I imagine
embracing each night

don't feel my arms wrap
around them

who's to say
they don't feel my breath

on their cheek
& know it's mine

Rain

I have spent years like this

hunched
against the frame

of the open door

silently
watching weather fall

into the space
prepared for it

& because language
has no utility here

sensation pares me

from the words
themselves

leaves me adrift
in this dusty porch

& I hope for neither
continuance

or change

shoulder tensed
against the wall

I try to merge
my mind

with the tilted shiver
of rain

that skips
over the pavement

the neighbours' tulips
shaking in the gloom

the bald stubble
of grass

with its half-coiled
cigarette butts

blooming open
in the water

like roses
in the ooze

sometimes
a downpour appears

in the distance

like a purl
of smoke

the dead flies astonished
back to life

as the rain finds our trash
& brings it

to our senses

juvenile shoots
pushing through

calcified cat shits
the crisp packets

& cracked lighters

at the entrance
to our home

where I stand here
most autumn

like a man

on the threshold
of heaven

Falls

wide-eyed
at the body's sudden arrival

each time
pressed against the edge

of catastrophe

the inevitability
of the ground

how the moment eats itself
sound dissolves

& the world is shaken new

the plastic cuff
of the crutch

jammed into the pit
of my arm

a grunt twisted from my lips

the pavement leaping
towards me

in a second that feels
like a slow-dripped hour

at thirteen

the bone in my foot
sang like a cymbal

when I slipped
down the staircase

& at eighteen

I was felled in the centre
of town

like a tree in a storm

each fall is a page
in a book

I flick open
in the quiet hours

reliving
the embarrassment & shock

the sound of teenage laughter
at the edges of the rain

the universe made
suddenly simple

The recurring dream

the son we're trying for
            turning somewhere

            in your mind

as flecks of gravel gleam
            through my lip

the applause of car-horns
            suspended in the air

a numbness climbs
            up my back

            in bed the width
            of a ghost

between your body & mine

            how I worry
            if my grip will ever fail

            blue eyes   tiny fingers
fumbling at my beard

            a curlicue of smoke
crawls over the road

            the drift of time
            of love between the sound

the crutch makes collapsing
            beneath me

& the weight of his still-
imagined form slipping

            from my hands

Father

there have been dreams

where I find you alone
& confused

dried blood threaded
in your brow

face bruised thick
as a lantern

& there have been dreams
where I search endlessly

for a sign
of your presence

worried for the safety
of the man who carried me

to bed from the car-seat
I would pretend to be asleep in

when you come to hold
your grandson

you tell me which
of your friends have died

why & how
unexpected it was

we balance the circumstances
& gauge the shock

their partners
their children must feel

as if pain
can be melted & weighed out

like gold

when night arrives
I listen

for the rasp of your cough
like a flint sparked

in the dark

the noises you make
when you jolt half-asleep

from our sofa-bed
the same as mine

we don't talk about this
coiling of time

how tightly our lives
are winding together

all those moments where you
have been my keeper

& I have been yours
as we dug each other out

of a place we won't talk about

a deep darkness where
we have been each other's father's

& we have been each other's son's

For the love of the Greenland shark

a perfume of thought brings
with it

the slow drip
of banks & turns

her eye fetched blue
the slick of blood

ripples like oil
in the wash

as she follows
the only journey she can

chasing one last spasm
of heat

blindly swimming

through three hundred years
of greenland salt

the scrapes & near misses

the memory
of a thousand tides

in her gills

body tumbled through
the surf

the same way a flaw splits a diamond
over centuries

somewhere
between smell & touch

her life spilled over
with presence

& what a privilege
of terror to be

the last thing embraced
between her jaws

a final thought held
in parenthesis

The leg

leaping over soft grass
or sand

in streets or fields
still carrying a human warmth

searching for the life
that left it

I once read a holy book say

our form
can not be spliced

& struck back together
after death

the soul of a partial body
will not carry through

even if made incomplete
by an ear even

a little finger
is enough to tear

that bond

there is a purgatory
for us

where hearts beat
their way through

the ocean's depth

jellyfish-like
one atrial squeeze at a time

the shoals of kidneys

& livers gliding slowly
through the half-light

chalk-dry hands
cracking

as they pull themselves
by the knuckles

over gravel desperate
for some puck of wholeness

looking for the homes
they have lost

& what kind of life could
this limb have lived with me ?

the mounting successes
& luck

or just the bliss
being either side

of the morning's first arc
of piss

Make-up

time has caught itself
in the creases of your cheeks

the fragments of mascara
& clumped foundation

I blot out
with the smallest turn of my hand

eyes closed

as I pull the glassy cleanser
over your brow

& the person I know best
starts to appear

like sunlight pooling
into an open room

& because your wrists ache
like baby teeth

cutting through the gum

this chore
has become an easy revelation

anyone could fall
in love with

this intimacy I perform
each night

when I kiss the lipstick
from your teeth

& miraculous
you appear from powder

& pigment
the seed of yourself

smiling
fastening your arms

around my neck

Adalimumab 40mg

the smell of hospital disinfectant
in your hair

& the box of needles shaking
in the boot

each tip of the new medication
as sharp

as fragile as the faith

that carries the dream
of remission into our lives

having fasted
under paper-thin sheets

for the last three days

you scald your lips
on fries

a pool of grease blooms

through the paper bag
like an exit wound

& the wrappers of our burgers
on the dashboard

unfasten
like the muscles of your thigh

that cinch then relax
over the bite of that first syringe

emptying a hope
that shivers

& burns

Spit

because what else
is there to do

in rooms
we can't afford to heat

than eat each other

the pulse of globules slick
& trembling

in the air

a trail of warmth traced
over your hip-bone

with my tongue
glistening

like all things

that have that clatter
of the sublime

about them

the hand
that clutches the ankle

the teeth
that graze the rib

the way
the headboard knocks

the shoulder

into a whorl
of blue confetti

the next day

the body keeps slipping
out of tune

& I just want

to be wrung through
with you

to tell you *low* isn't unholy

& currency
isn't the only tender

we can honour
between fingers

lips

breath to breast
& tongue to neck

this rope we climb

Deserted carpark

the silhouette
of a sunflower lit

by our headlights
& swaying against

the concrete wall
of the deserted carpark

as you go down on me
in your best dress

in the passenger seat
I light two cigarettes

in an alternate world
& pass you one

to thread smoke
through the gap

of your window
in another

I am the driver
you the passenger

or I am the sunflower
watching on

with a yellow curiosity
the only noise

spilling through
the heart of this half-

finished building
our shallow breath

& the low voices
on the radio

diggers left to rust
in perfect rows

& cherry-pickers
stalled mid-gesture

as though
they are lifting up

the cool half-dark
my calf eases against

the buckled glovebox
spilling parking tickets

& tissue packets
onto the floor

as everywhere
the evening sinks

towards its final form

Making love for cripples

we keep waking inside the notion
of bodies in love

how one broken person

slides their tongue
into another

until there is nothing left

of the sadness or shame
that otherwise

divides them

this is the light
I choose to tilt over the world

arrested each morning

by the flinch of asymmetry
that leaps from the mirror

the only way I can leave

is to cup the tinder
of your body close

enough to feel its warmth

& far enough
to let it catch

like the fragile mosses
of the soil

falling over each other
in a century of yearning

the drifting corals
burning into brightness

to inhabit the moment
without knowing it

to break the spell
of its looking

Still life, in bed

I haven't touched you like this
for months

the half-emptied jar of coconut oil
on the headboard

& our finger-marks gouged
in the surface

those lumps of pale grease
like fish

floating behind the glass

when I watch you
raise your left hip

as you stand at the skillet

hot oil leaping into the air
like a plea

something inside me comes loose

the notion
of your warm hands

the way your body turns
in the light

the gap between your upper lip
& the outline

of your nostril

I have been falling
into the first inhalation

that caught in my chest

the moment I saw you
a decade ago

it has held the hand

of each consecutive
breath since

& still   you turn into me
in joy & pain

because that's what love is

falling always
into the soft mirror

of the other

Anniversary

shadows flicker against the glass

as rain batters the skylight
above us in bed

tomorrow's outfits
hung over

the wardrobe door

a pair of ghosts
waiting to be occupied

by another version
of us

the spasm of lightning

& thunder
rolling its applause

over this half-decade
we've built

our life into

I still measure your unlikeliness
in the sheets

as you sleep

the pallor of your skin
the angle that cuts

your hip to your waist

this history I carry
behind my eyes

threatening to spill over
it all

when goosebumps ripple over
your chest

I press my ear to it
like a receiver

& let our story
run through me

again & again

how the first summer
smelt of pollen

& the bloodied sheets

from the awkward music
our bodies

strained to make

five years
& we've learnt to stop

asking questions
of the future

Ovulation cycle twenty-one

we both keep this lie
between us

praying each month
that your period will fail

only for it to arrive
once again

constant as the moon

surely as the pain
that keeps us here

we guard this lazy faith
in our fertility

& because words are too precise

sharp enough to tear
this fragile future

we've knitted
into the air

maybe the child that breathes
between the sheets

of our dreams

is a placeholder
for the fantasy

of a normal life
we empty

our trust into

can almost feel
against our fingertips

Ovulation cycle twenty-two

we track your periods

in the calendar
on our kitchen wall

turn the page each month

as each month
the tissue pulls away

to spiral through the bowl
of the toilet

a tiny ghost

our sadness gathers
over each fresh thimble

of blood

every few days
you peel the glossy wrapper

from an ovulation strip
& sit half-asleep in the bathroom

pissing
through the dark

the tap running into shadow

as I tell you my dream
from the other room

resting against the root of a tree
whose trunk reached miles

beyond my sight
an apple fell

it swallowed the distance
towards me

as I listened to the air

guessing the moment
the direction I must dive

to catch it
before it hits the ground

I tossed my whole life
towards this unknowable arc

& rolling over a dusty turf
of bruised & dripping fruit

I opened my fist
over nothing

What you carry

fingertips hum
above the screen

turning over a page
of suspended light

on your kindle
as quiet

as the stitch of iron
threaded inside you

from the transparent bags of iv
hung in the air

like the half-dead goldfish

we would win
at the fair

& those fragile globes of plastic
that held them

the envelope between
life & death

slim as the tip of the needle
that the surface of your vein

resists for a moment
before it slides through

how the baby inside you
sends your blood pressure

vaulting

& the blades
of the speculum bloom

open

your lashes sticky
with tears

when the thin beak
nicks the lip

of your cervix

all the ways
the world has travelled

into your body

all the ways
the world has pushed

against the edge
of your form

hand on belly

the incomprehensible beating
inside you

Scan

your tiny femur echoes a signal
back to the screen

you have haunted us
for months

seeded
in every thought

we considered you for years
before we even started

trying
to bring you to life

heart a pale balloon
inflating with pixels

still more alien
than anything

no more your mother than me
somehow asleep

beneath the folds of fluid
in the bony pubis

I can make out
the channels of your nose

the pale blade
of your tibia

on the monitor

the panic in me swimming
in each pause

before this stranger
at the screen says

here you are

Heatwave, 2022

on the hottest day on record
the line went blue

we barely lifted
a finger

that afternoon

we'd been waiting weeks
for the rain

to slit the sky in two

like the belly
of some vast animal

for the cool air to stretch
over us

like a pair of wings

we checked the strip
again & again

dripping with sweat
on the sofa

we watched
the pixelated weather shift

on your phone

the yellow sun growing dark
as vinegar

the first patter of rain streaking

into thick veins
against the glass

the death card unshipped
from the deck twice

that month

checking each sheet
of toilet paper

for that same red gloss

that visited us
six weeks in

I made you peppermint tea at 4am

rubbed oil
into your expanding belly

each night

then the sides of your breasts
until the ducts filled

that first drop of milk
pale as ice-water

the heat turned to rain
the seasons turned

& we sat perfectly
in the seats of our reality

for once pain was not our god

whatever this was
it was the opposite

Acknowledgements

Many thanks to the BBC for commissioning 'Atopic Dermatitis' for their centenary, and thank you to the editors of *Bad Lillies, Modron, Ink, Sweat and Tears* and *Poetry Wales* where some of these poems appeared first.

I am incredibly appreciative to the friends, peers, and fellow writers who have helped me with feedback on some of these poems, especially Harriet Jae, Jamie Field, Dr Dorothy Lehane, Isabel Galleymore, Rachael Boast, Matthew Siegel and Carrie Etter.

I am greatly indebted to Jane Commane and Angela Hicken, for their continued support and enthusiasm in bringing another book to fruition with Nine Arches Press.

For the time and space to write this book, whilst co-parenting and dealing with pain and disability, I am immensely grateful to my wife, Emily. I couldn't do any of this without you.